Flavel Bascom, Frederic T Perkins

A Historical Discourse Commemorative of the Settlement of

Galesburg

Delivered in the First Church of Galesburg, June 22, 1866

Flavel Bascom, Frederic T Perkins

A Historical Discourse Commemorative of the Settlement of Galesburg
Delivered in the First Church of Galesburg, June 22, 1866

ISBN/EAN: 9783337003906

Printed in Europe, USA, Canada, Australia, Japan

Cover: Foto ©ninafisch / pixelio.de

More available books at **www.hansebooks.com**

A

HISTORICAL DISCOURSE:

COMMEMORATIVE OF THE

SETTLEMENT OF GALESBURG.

DELIVERED IN THE FIRST CHURCH OF GALESBURG,

JUNE 22, 1866.

By REV. FLAVEL BASCOM,
A FORMER PASTOR OF THE CHURCH.

AND

A STATISTICAL PAPER:

By REV. FREDERIC T. PERKINS,
PRESENT PASTOR OF THE CHURCH.

GALESBURG, ILL.
FREE PRESS BOOK AND JOB PRINTING HOUSE.
1866.

THE ladies of the First Church in Galesburg, remembering all the way in which the Lord had led their Pioneer Fathers and Mothers, resolved to commemorate the settlement of the place. The notice of the proposed celebration, published in the FREE PRESS of June 17th, through the Chairman of their committee, Miss M. A. WEST, contains the following state. ment:

"The First Church of this city propose commemorating the settlement of Galesburg by a "Historical Celebration on the 22d day of June. Thirty years ago this month, Galesburg "was founded by a noble band of men and women, who left home and friends in the East, not "in search of wealth, but simply to do good, by founding a village and a school, which should "be lights in a dark place.

"One by one these fathers and mothers are passing from us; with them will die very much "that is valuable of the early history of this place.

"We deem it therefore a duty to collect this history now while we may, for their names "and the memory of their deeds we would not willingly let die."

In preparing for the celebration, they engaged the Rev. FLAVEL BASCOM—a former pastor of the church—to deliver a Historical Discourse, and the Rev. F. T. PERKINS—the present pastor—to prepare a Statistical Paper, respecting the growth and business of the city. At the appointed time—June 22d, 1866—a congregation of old settlers and others gathered in the First Church, at 3 o'clock P. M., and listened to the following Discourse and Paper.

HISTORICAL DISCOURSE.

Colonization has always been one of God's Providential agencies for peopling the earth, and promoting a better civilization. Emigration has its disadvantages and dangers. Solitary families removing from the precincts of Christian civilization, into regions destitute of religious and educational Institutions, are liable to grow indifferent to learning and religion, and to drift in the direction of barbarism. This dangerous tendency is fully illustrated in the state of society in some sections of our Western country, where, remote from the atmosphere of social refinement, intellectual culture, and religious sentiment, people that once had higher aspirations, have ceased to think of those things which are pure and lovely and of good report, and have become grovelling in their tastes, dissolute in their sentiments, and godless in their lives.

But organized ~~civilization~~ aims to carry the influences of Christian civilization into new communities and to plant there the germs of religious and educational institutions, which shall spring up and keep progress with the growth of society, and ultimately fill the community with their precious fruits. If this can be done, the evils of solitary emigration are not only avoided, but some advantages are gained of great value. Evils exist in old communities, and to remedy them is not easy. Public sentiment is there conservative of wrong as well as right, customs are stereotyped, and ·he who sets himself to put away existing evils and reform so-

ciety, needs a power that can remove mountains.   But where
a new community is planted on virgin soil, it is easier to
commence right, and form the sentiment and the habits of
that community in conformity to right principles.   The old
shackles of custom are more easily broken, and old abuses
discarded.

When God therefore, as if despairing of bringing the
whole race forward together in a process of intellectual and
religious culture, called Abraham, with a small select company from Ur, of the Chaldees, to go into Canaan, his object
was by establishing a new community there, to secure an
improved state of society, and raise up a community that
should be the salt of the earth.   It would be easy to show
from history that by organized emigration, the arts and
sciences, the blessings of civil liberty and true religion have
been propagated in the world and preserved in all ages.   The
settlement of New England by Christian Colonies from
Great Britain is an ever memorable example of the glorious
possibilities of good from this instrumentality.   Not only
were important towns, and settlements, and churches built
up by original colonies from the old world, but these settlements were ever sending out new colonies from themselves,
to people new towns, and build up all the institutions of
civilized and Christian communities.   It was this mode of
settlement, under the blessing of God, that made New England what it is, in intelligence and piety.   And thus New
England has been able to furnish no small portion of the
intelligence and sterling moral principle that has saved the
nation.

It is not surprising that the descendants of the Pilgrims
should have been inclined to settle the valley of the Missis
sippi by colonies.   In this way early settlements were made
in Ohio, which were eminently successful, e. g., at Marietta
on the south, and in many localities on the reserve.   In
this section of our own State, numerous colonies from
different Eastern States were planted from twenty-five to

thirty-five years ago, with different objects and various degrees of success. Princeton was founded by a colony from Hampshire and Hamden counties, Massachusetts. Wethersfield and Andover were colonies from Connecticut. Tremont and Delaware were colonies from Boston and Providence. Other places less prominent had a similar origin. But the Galesburg colony has always maintained a pre-eminence among kindred enterprises, and has achieved a success which no other has yet attained. I account for this fact mainly on two principles: 1st. The object of this colony was prominently and distinctively philanthropic, benevolent and Christian. Its founders designed to water others, and God has watered them. They aimed to plant a Christian community, to maintain a high-toned Christian morality, and they found that godliness was profitable unto all things having the promise of the life that now is, as well as of that which is to come. 2d. The plan of this colony was more complete. Its affairs were systematized, with a wise adaptation of means to the end in view.

An enterprise with such an object and such a plan, attracted to itself a class of men who could appreciate its importance, and were able to carry out its design, without faltering, or turning aside. Such men engaged in such a work, are in the way to secure God's blessing, for they are laborers together with him. In this view of the case the prosperity of Galesburg and of its inhabitants is no marvel. Let other communities learn from it the secret of success.

It is thirty years this month, since the earliest pioneers of this colony arrived with their families and commenced those labors which in the meantime have changed a desert into a populous city, distinguished for its religious and literary institutions, and commercial prosperity. It is a fitting time for the surviving founders of such institutions and of such a community, to commemorate the laying of their foundations, and to set up their monument to the praise of Him who hitherto hath helped them.

The conception of this enterprise originated, as is well known, with the Rev. George W. Gale, then residing in Oneida county, New York. Mr. Gale had been connected with the Oneida Institute, in which many valuable young men had been put forward in a course of study, toward the ministry, and he had become deeply interested in providing more ample means for the christian education of the youth of both sexes, in order to meet the wants of our country and the world. He conferred with his brethren, and was strengthened by their approval and aided by their suggestions. As early as 1834 he seems to have matured a well developed plan for planting a colony at the West, to be a center of intellectual and moral illumination. In speaking of the motives by which he and his associates were educated, Mr. Gale says: "Their views were not restricted to benefitting their own descendants. The object which gave birth to the enterprize was that of diffusing over an important region of country, at an early period of its settlement, the combined influence of education and religion."

The plan of the colony was a remarkable combination of philanthropy and sagacity. It was based upon the assumption that the religious, educational and social advantages which the plan contemplated, would greatly enhance the value of the wild lands in the vicinity of their town. These lands were to be purchased by the colony at the government price, and sold to individual members or other purchasers at four times their first cost, and the profit thus accruing was to endow their College in its various departments. And the purchaser of every eighty acre lot received a scholarship entitling the holder to twenty-five years' tuition.

The original design was to raise by subscription, $40,000, and purchase a whole township. If this amount had been raised and a whole township purchased at Government price, it would have still left more than $11,000 in the Treasury for College purposes, and when the subscribers had all received their lands at an average of $5 per acre, it would have left 15,000 acres of land as the property of the College. The town site was also to be located on College land, which would of itself furnish no inconsiderable endowment for an infant institution.

The unquestionable wisdom of the plan is demonstrated by the fact, that, although but about one-half of the sum originally contemplated was ever received from subscribers, and only 10,746 acres of land purchased for the colony, yet on this greatly diminished scale of operations, the enterprise has proved eminently successful.

In the summer of 1835, about thirty subscribers to the plan of a colony having been obtained, an exploring Committee was appointed, consisting of Nehemiah West, Thomas Gilbert, and Timothy B. Jervis. They spent some months in traveling through the West, particularly in Northern Indiana and Northern Illinois, and returned without being able to recommend any location as fully meeting the wishes and plans of the colony. They were, however, favorably impressed with this section of Illinois, and believed that in this vicinity a suitable tract of land might be found. One of the Committee purchased a farm for himself in the vicinity of Knoxville, feeling confident that the colony would purchase around him. The Committee recommended that a purchasing Committee be immediately sent out, prepared to make further explorations and secure by actual purchase the most suitable tract of land they could find in this part of the State. That Committee was appointed, consisting of Rev. Mr. Gale, Sylvanus Ferris, Nehemiah West, and Thomas Simmons, who soon set out on their important mission. At Detroit they were obliged to leave Mr. Gale on account of his illness, and Mr. Samuel Tompkins, who was in company with one of the Committee, was requested to act in Mr. Gale's place. The Committee arrived at Knoxville about the middle of October, 1835, and their attention was soon directed to this tract of prairie, adjacent to the South, side of Henderson Grove which the exploring Committee seem not to have visited. They decided at once to purchase it in connection with two improved farms, and a tract of timber in the grove. The money invested in the purchase fell a little short of $15,000.

On the 7th of the succeeding January, 1836, the stock-holders of the colony met at Whitesboro, heard the report of their Committee, and appointed a Board of Trustees of their embryo College, consisting of John Waters, Sylvanus Ferris, H. H. Kellogg, Thomas Simmons, John C. Smith, Walter Webb, G. W. Gale, N. West, Isaac Mills, and Samuel Tompkins.

" Prairie College " was selected as the name of their institution, and Galesburg the name of the village.— Arrangements were made for appraising the lands, and distributing them to the stockholders and selling to new purchasers; for laying out the village, and appraising the lots and bringing them into market, reserving College grounds, and lots for a Church, a parsonage and a Cemetery. Steps were taken toward procuring at an early day, material for a College building, the erection of a steam saw-mill and of a public house.

As early in the Spring of 1836 as arrangements could be made, the Pioneers of the Colony began their long and weary pilgrimage to the land of promise; a part with their own teams, and a part by water, in their own canal boat through the New York and Erie canal from Utica to Buffalo; on Lake Erie to Cleveland; by the Ohio canal to Portsmouth; thence by the Ohio, Mississippi and Illinois rivers to Copperas Creek, the landing nearest to their destination. The voyage was long, their progress was slow, the boat was crowded, the weather was warm, the alternations of scorching heat by day, and chilly dampness by night, necessarily subjected them to sickness, which very few if any escaped. Three died early after their arrival, Smith, Mills, and Lyman, strong men, valuable in counsel and efficient in labors. Their loss was deeply felt, their survivors were afflicted but not discouraged, cast down, but not in despair. They were well aware that men die, but God lives and his cause does not fail.

In the autumn of 1836 more than thirty families were temporarily located in cabins on the South side of Henderson Grove, where they spent the first winter preparing to improve their farms, and to commence the building of their village the next season. Then and there was planted the germ of this city with its noble institutions, and of the thriving community by which the city is surrounded. Had a Directory of Log City (as their temporary settlement was called) been published that winter, it would have contained the following names: Geo. Avery, H. T. Avery, M. Chambers, L. Chappel, C. S. Colton, H. Conger, L. E. Conger, P. Dunn, Geo. Ferris, H. Ferris, C. Finch, Rev. Geo. W. Gale, L. Gay, D. Griffith. A. Goodell, Wm. Hamblin, J. Haskins, Mrs. Hitchcock, A. Kendall, J. Kendall, E. H. King, N. H. Losey, H. Lyman, J. Mills, J. McMullen, R. Payne, Mrs. Phelps, Philemon Phelps, P. Richardson, R. Root, J. Simmons, T. Simmons, J. C. Smith, E. Swift, Job. Swift, S. Tompkins, A. Tyler, Rev. J. Waters, D. Wheeler, J. G. West, N. West, H. Wilcox.

The Spring of 1837 witnessed the arrival of B. Allen, D. Allen, N. Allen, S. Allen, F. Buckingham, Dr. J. Bunce, I. Colton, E. Farnham, S. Ferris, N. O. Ferris, Wm. Ferris, W. Holyoke, A. Martin, H. H. May, J. C. Prentice, L. Sanderson, R. Skinner. Other families came in the autumn of 1837, but the families and individuals named above founded the colony.

And now commenced in earnest the stern, long protracted labors and trials, incident to the building up of such a community in such circumstances, labors and trials that can never be appreciated but by actual experience. The majority of the first settlers had but limited pecuniary resources, and these were soon swallowed up in current family expenses, in building their houses and improving their farms. In the meantime, that memorable financial crash had occurred, which involved the whole country and especially the West in the greatest embarrassment. Business was stagnant; farmers produce was a drug in the market and would scarcely pay for transportation. Markets were distant, and for a considerable portion of the year quite inaccessable. Privation, in respect to very many of the comforts of life, was therefore unavoidable. Money was so exceedingly difficult to be obtained for anything the settlers had to spare, that they became accustomed to its absence, and learned to transact most kinds of business without it. They were exceedingly accommodating in their traffic with each other. Great ingenuity was developed in the barter of their commodities, and where this failed, long credits contributed to their convenience. But for taxes and postage, neither the barter nor credit system would answer, and often letters from distant loved ones were suffered to remain a considerable time in the post-office for the want of twenty-five cents, which was then the postage on all our Eastern correspondence.

The first goods were sold in the settlement by Mr. C. S. Colton, who opened at the Grove in 1836, on a scale corresponding to the size of the infant community. The next year he removed his store to the village, on the West side of the Public Square, and on the North of Main street he built his store and dwelling under the same roof. In that building, for almost a score of years, a growing mercantile business was conducted; remunerative to the proprietor and at the same time a great convenience to the community. But only those of my hearers who remember what it was to go a shopping in Galesburg in those early times can realize the difference between then and now. The advantage, in some respects, was certainly on the side of those times. The merchant was better satisfied, for he had but little competition and large profits. And the customer had much less difficulty in satisfying himself that he had found the best article in town. That could speedily be done. He was not expected to pay anything down for his purchases. No matter how low his funds were, he need not go empty away. Goods were to be had without money, if not without price. As to price, the pioneer merchants of the West sometimes claimed that they made but one per cent. profit. What they bought for one dollar they sold for two, and that was gaining one dollar on every hundred cents. And what customer could grudge them so small a profit, when pay-day was so distant? But alas! those pay days, however long delayed, would come, and their approach was not among the smallest trials of pioneer life.

In their social feelings and habits, the early settlers of Galesburg were exceedingly free and cordial. Though many of them had been strangers to each other till they were brought together here, they were so homogeneous in their principles and aims as to inspire mutual confidence and fraternal attachment from their first acquaintance. Then there were no classes of society, and no artificial rules of etiquette to restrain the freedom of social intercourse. No particular style of living was requisite to admission into the best society. If a family had not chairs enough to seat their guests, this was no obstacle to their receiving and entertaining company. Boxes, trunks and benches made convenient seats, and who need be ashamed of such furniture, when it was the fashion in the best of families.

There is something in pioneer life which binds the early settlers to each other in very strong attachments. Their hardships and privations teach them to sympathize with each other and their mutual dependence trains them to habits of mutual helpfulness. I was once told by an Illinoisan who was a native of Kentucky, that he had settled three new countries and had seen all sorts of society, and the best society to be found anywhere was among the earliest pioneers of a settlement. They lived on bear's flesh and bread made of pounded corn, and neighbors were so distant that they knew how to prize them. All were equal and all were friendly. But, said he, as soon as they get flour bread and meat of their own raising, they begin to be proud and envious, they quarrel and have law-suits, and there is no more good society. Probably his theory of good society was somewhat radical and extreme, but like other radical ideas his had true philosophy in them.

A prominent object of the projector and members of the colony was the founding of an institution of learning, which should afford the best advantages for a thoroughly Christian education in its various departments, at the lowest practicable expense to the pupils. This object they never lost sight of for a moment. Their earliest efforts were directed toward the accomplishment of this part of their plan. The first winter, while yet occupying the rude cabins of "Log City," with such accommodations as they could furnish, a school was taught by a gentleman and lady, both in the common and academic branches. A charter for the institution was obtained the same winter from our State Legislature under the name of "Knox Manual Labor College." Immediate steps were taken for the erection of an Academy building, which was completed in the fall of 1838, and opened for students early in the succeeding winter with more than thirty pupils. In 1838 Mr. Kellogg was appointed President of the institution, Mr. Gale, Professor of Rhetoric and Moral Philosophy, and Mr. Losey, who had hitherto conducted the Preparatory department, Professor of Mathematics and Natural sciences. In 1841 the College was fully organized and a promising class entered on their Freshman year. Mr. Grant, in the meantime having been appointed Professor of Languages. In 1843 the institution met with a severe loss by fire. Their building which had been erected for the special benefit of the Female department, at an expense of more than $5,000, was burned, without insurance. In 1844 the East College building was erected, and the West College the year following, after the same plan. Besides the Lecture and Recitation rooms, Library, etc., these two buildings were designed to accommodate about forty students with rooms for study. In 1850 both these buildings were enlarged and their accommodations greatly improved at a considerable expense. In 1857 the Central College building and Female Seminary were built at an expense of about $80,000. At that time the whole endowment of the institution was estimated at not less than $400,000, and all the donations it had received from sources outside of the colony had been scarcely $50,-000. In 1845 Mr. Kellogg retired from the Presidency and Mr. Blanchard succeeded him. Under his administration the first class of nine young men was graduated, five of whom became ministers, two of these foreign missionaries, two physicians, one Professor in College and one farmer. In 1851 the first class of three graduated from the Female Collegiate department, a three years' course of study having been provided for under the instruction of the College Faculty, with Professor Hitchcock and a Female Principal devoted wholly to this department. This department has compared favorably with the other in numbers and schollarship, and has fully justified the wisdom of the founders of the College in providing with like liberality for the education of both sexes.

Previous to the last financial disaster in 1857, the College had attained to very great prosperity. The value of its endowment far surpassed the most sanguine expectations of its founders. The intersection of two important Railroads at this point had so stimulated all kinds of business as to attract a large population, and transform a small interior village into a flourishing city. This brought the College lands into requisition and greatly enhanced their value. Valuable lands which were originally appropriated conditionally to a Theological Seminary, by the failure of that condition, reverted to the general funds of the College. In the meantime the Railroad Depot having been located upon their border, those lands became city lots, and were sold by the foot instead of the acre. The reputation which the place had acquired by the character of its society, and of its Religious and Literary institutions attracted a class of population which had in themselves the elements of thrift and prosperity. And while the College shared largely in the general prosperity, it contributed no less to promote it.

The establishment of a Theological Seminary as a part of the Educational System of this place, was prevented by a plan long since formed, and not yet realized by our Presbyterian brethren, of building up a Denominational Seminary at Galena. Thence the location was changed to Chicago or Lake Forest, and finally, I believe, to Carlinville, to which place it was invited by the prospect of endowment from lands secured at an early day by Dr. Blackburn. The Manual Labor feature of the College proved to be less valuable than was anticipated. A few of the early pupils aided themselves to some extent by Horticultural and Mechanical labors. But experience, the surest test of theories, did not justify a reliance upon the labors of the pupils during term time, as their chief resource for defraying their expenses. Manual labor therefore gradually fell into neglect, and finally was dropped from the name of the institution by an amendment of the charter.

The faith and patience, and self-denial with which the

Faculty of the College struggled through the long years of poverty and trial, which covered at least one half of its history, commend them to the lasting gratitude of all the friends of Christian education. Their nominal salaries were very inadequate, and these were generally largely in arrears. When paid they were sometimes in College Scrip, which was current only at a considerable discount. But God gave them endurance and brought them through their straits into a large place, and rewarded them for all their sacrifices. And now their works follow them in the precious fruits gathered from the seed they sowed. The able scholars, the earnest and efficient men and women whom they instructed, are now conferring manifold blessings upon the world by their influence. The early classes in the institution, were of like spirit with their teachers, and in full sympathy with the principles and objects of the colony. Long may this spirit and these principles be cherished among the successive generations of pupils that shall walk these classic halls; and never may the public sentiment of the College cease to be in harmony with the objects and ends for which the colony was founded.

How inadequate the idea entertained by most people of the magnitude of the work of founding a College. In the early settlements of the West almost every colony and nearly every ambitious town, aspired to be a seat of learning; and many were the charters obtained for Colleges, with the expectation apparently that they would grow as spontaneously as a tree, when once planted. Not long since, a town not a hundred miles from here, advertised itself as a very eligible site for a College. Through its local weekly newspaper it informed the world that if any person desired to build a College, they would do well to examine the advantages of that locality before selecting any other site, as if the building up of a College was like establishing a store, or erecting a manufactory, or starting a newspaper.

No one that has not tried it, can conceive of the outlay of faith, patience, toil, care, and money demanded in making up a well ordered and adequately endowed College. Society little knows how much it is indebted to those who have done such a work. There are men now in this community, and some have passed away, who have for a long series of years borne burdens of care, solicitude and responsibility in looking after the finances, and other material interests of this College, for which money could but poorly compensate them. And yet they have done it without fee or commission, and ometimes without thanks. May God reward them.

There have graduated from the male department of Knox College, 131. Of these 38 became Ministers, 3 Foreign Missionaries, 24 Lawyers, and quite a number Professors and Teachers. One hundred and eighteen have graduated from the Female Collegiate department, many of whom are filling stations of great usefulness in society. The aggregate of the names found on the catalogues of the academic department during the period of its existence, is 7687. Of whom almost one-half have been females.

But, as many of the pupils continue through several years and the same names appear in several successive catalogues, it is estimated that but about 5,000 differrent persons have been instructed for a longer or shorter period in some of the departments of the institution. The good influences thus put forth in operation are widely diffused, and are acting on society at points distant from each other and in manifold ways. The infinite mind alone can comprehend the results. About one-third of the gentlemen graduates, and not far from the same proportion of the young gentlemen connected at different times with the Academy, have performed valuable military service to their country in the late rebellion. Not one so far as is known has fought against his country.

A most unhappy strife in the Board of Trustees for some years circumscribed the usefulness of the institution, and brought all its interests into peril. But the storm has spent its fury and the College still lives, we trust to bless the world through a long series of unborn generations. Let the friends of the institution learn wisdom from their experience, and henceforth strive only to secure the great ends of its founders; the promotion of sound learning, scriptural morality, and pure religion,

Time will doubtless convince us all, as it already has some of us, that the strife grew not out of wicked designs, so much as of human infirmities, that the provocation was not all on one side, nor the forbearance and purity of motive monopolized by one party. In the meantime, a second institution of learning, not on the programme of the colony, has sprung into existence, and has attained to a good degree of prosperity and an influential position in the State. The Universalists in this place and vicinity, encouraged by the liberal donations of their friends abroad, and especially of B. Lombard, Esq., established Lombard University in 1852. They have an able Faculty, and one good building well filled with pupils. The institution is for both sexes.

Galesburg has also introduced the system of Graded Public Schools, and by providing able teachers, and erecting a noble building, evinces a determination to educate the whole population.

In the infant settlement at "Log City," public worship on the Sabbath was established very soon after the arrival of the first families, with preaching when practicable. Mr. Gale was their first stated supply. Assisted by Rev. John T. Avery, he held a series of meetings during the first winter, and the spirit of God owned and blessed the effort in the conversion of several of the youth in the congregation. They organized their Church on the 25th of February, 1836, consisting of eighty-two members. Mr. Waters and Mr. Gale officiated on the occasion, assisted by Mr. Noel, of Knoxville, who represented Schuyler Presbytery. The

Church was Presbyterian in its name and ecclesiastical rela-
tions, but contained a strong Congregational element, out of
deference to which, the modes of administering its affairs,
were somewhat modified, from the beginning.

During the summer of 1837, some families having prepared residences in the village removed hither, and then
public worship was held alternately, here and at the grove.
The first room used for Sabbath worship in Galesburg, was
a store-room built by Deacon Chambers, on Main street
and afterward used for mercantile purposes. In the winter of
1839 the first Academy building was used for religious meetings, which were thenceforward constantly held there until
this house was opened for worship in 1846.   The seven years
in which the Church worshiped in the old Academy were
memorable as a period of spiritual prosperity and almost
constant progress.   Many were the seasons of refreshing
from the presence of the Lord there enjoyed, and of not a
few now in Heaven, and of many on their way thither, it
may be said, "this and that man was born there."   Although
worship was commenced in this house in the summer of
1846, it was not finished and dedicated till the beginning of
1848.   For some three years after this it was the only house
for public worship in the village, and Christians of every
denomination were accustomed to worship together here·
In 1851 the adjoining Lecture room was built; which has
been a great convenience for social worship, for a session
room and for meetings of general interest, but miscellaneous
in character.

Professor Gale, with the aid of Rev. Mr. Waters, was
acting pastor of the Church the first three years.   Mr.
Foote supplied the pulpit for one year.   Mr. Gale then
resumed his pastoral labors for a year, and was succeeded by
President Kellogg, who was stated supply for two years.
For the next year the pulpit was supplied by Rev. Messrs.
Marsh, Waters, and Hollister.   From May 1844 till the end

of 1845, Rev. Mr. Parker was acting pastor. Mr. Kellogg then was installed as pastor, and officiated till the failure of his health in the spring of 1847. President Blanchard succeeded him in his ministerial and pastoral labors, and gave place to Mr. Bascom in December, 1849, whose pastorate closed in May, 1856. His successor was Rev. Charles M. Tyler, whose pastoral relation to the Church continued about three years. Mr. Barnard was then stated supply for six months, and was succeeded by the present pastor, Rev. F. T. Perkins, who already lacks but little of having reached the length of the longest pastorate which had preceded his. Long may it be before history shall give us the name of his successor. If the Church has not been edified by the ministry of these thirty years, surely it has not been for the lack of variety.

In 1845 the government of the Church was modified and an accommodation plan adopted, which secured to both Congregationalists and Presbyterians their preferences, and gave the Church a double ecclesiastical connection. In 1856 the term Presbyterian was dropped from her name, and she has since been known as the first Church of Christ, having withdrawn from Presbytery a year or two before. In May, 1854, the second Presbyterian Church was organized with thirty members, dismissed from this Church for this purpose; and in December of the same year the Old School Presbyterian Church was organized with eighteen members. In November, 1855, the first Congregational Church was organized with fifty members, most of whom were dismissed from this Church to join the new organization.

The Methodist Episcopal Church, the Baptist and the Swedish Evangelical Lutheran were organized in the order now named, in 1847, 1848 and 1852. In October, 1856, a Swedish Methodist and also a Colored Methodist Church were organized and subsequently an Episcopal Church, a German Lutheran, a Colored Baptist, and a Roman Catho-

lic.   A Universalist Church has also held a somewhat
prominent position in the place for about twelve or fifteen years. Thus we see, while this spacious house of
worship met the wants of all Galesburg fifteen years ago,
fourteen houses, several of which are spacious and handsome
edifices, are now demanded.   If such increased church
accommodations are really needed and filled, it indicates a
degree of growth and prosperity, both temporal and
spiritual, which is rarely witnessed.

  This Church truly deserves to be called the Mother of
Churches, and of some of her offspring she may well be
proud, while some of the younger generation around her,
would probably prefer to trace their lineage to a source more
remote, if not more illustrious.   The present membership
of the Church is 362, still making her a little larger, as
she always ought to be, than any of her descendants.

  This Church has always been self-sustaining.   Though
planted in a new and uncultivated missionary field, her relation has always been that of a nursing mother to the feebler
and more destitute, rather than a recipient of other's bounty.

  This Church and colony have from the beginning taken
high and unequivocal ground on the questions of Reform
which have agitated the nation.   The original colony and
the early settlers were of one heart and one mind, in
this respect.   At their meeting in Whitesboro, the winter
before the settlement was begun, a committee, consisting of
Smith, West, and Tompkins, was appointed to report what
measures should be taken to guard the morals of the colony.
I do not find a formal report of this committee, but I do find
that a prohibition of the manufacture and sale of intoxicating drinks on the premises, is inserted in every title deed of
real estate, sold by the colony, and forfeiture to the College
is the penalty of violating that condition.   I infer that this
very important safe-guard to the morals of Galesburg was
thus early recommended by that committee.   Wise fore-
thought!   Precious legacy to those that shall come after

them ! Let Galesburg prize the precious inheritance received from the founders of the place, of exemption from the curse of the Liquor traffic ; and let her hand down to coming generations, that inheritance unsullied. Shame on the descendants or successors of such men as founded this colony, that shall ever consent to sell their birth-right of Temperance, and of uncompromising hostility to the Liquor traffic. Total abstinence from intoxicating drinks and opposition to slavery have been a condition of membership in this Church from the beginning.

The members and the ministry of this Church have always been in favor of carrying radical anti-slavery principles into politics as well as into religion. They have insisted on voting as well as praying for liberty. And she has done what she could to save the country, and give liberty to her oppressed millions, not only by her prayers and votes, but by sending into the army her full quota of brave soldiers who knew how to fight the battles of freedom.

It only remains now to address a few words of congratulation to the surviving founders of Galesburg and of its noble institutions. My friends, yours has been a favored lot. It was a kind Providence that chose you for such a work as God has permitted you here to accomplish. You have been benefactors of your country and of mankind. Not only this community, but the world owes you a debt of gratitude for the moral heroism with which you gave yourselves to this work ; for the faith and patience with which you prosecuted it ; for the self-denial and fortitude with which you endured hardness, as good soldiers of Jesus Christ.

You have not forgotten, and we will not forget, the long years in which you had to labor and wait for the realization of your hopes. The early history of your enterprise seemed a day of small things ; hope was often deferred ; embarrassments, trials and discouragements were multiplied and prolonged. But the bow of promise always spanned your sky, and hope was an anchor to your souls. The leaders and

prominent actors in your enterprize are worthy of great
praise; but they deserve not all the honor; it is the rank
and file in the army which receive and give the hard blows
that bring the victory.   And so it has been with the toiling
farmers, the industrious mechanics, and the patient and work-
ing housewives, that have fought the battles of this thirty
years' struggle, and achieved the victory which we celebrate
to-day.   I congratulate you on your success; and in the name
of the community, and of the thousands who have shared
the advantages of your institutions, I thank you for all you
have done and suffered for their benefit.   And in your
behalf, I thank God that he has spared you to this day to witness the results of your enterprise.   Did I say results? Ah!
these are not yet developed.   What we see and rejoice in
to-day are only some of the first fruits; the full harvest will
be reaped by successive generations, long after you have
gone.   And the full value of the results can be known only
in eternity.   But beware my friends, that you cherish not
the spirit that says: "This is great Babylon that I have
built."   Remember always, that he that planteth is nothing,
and he that watereth is nothing, but God that giveth the
increase.   To God belongs all the glory of your achievements.
    Many with whom you started this enterprise, are not
here to-day.   You cherish their memory with unusual ten-
derness and affection ; you went with them to the house of
God, and took sweet counsel with them in the days of dark-
ness and trial ; and you rejoiced with them in seasons of prosperity and of spiritual refreshing.   Would that time would
permit me to speak fitting words of eulogy for each.   But it
is not needful; their very names recall the history of their
lives, and their best eulogies are your memories of what
they were.   Smith, Mills, and Lyman, fell on the threshold
of your enterprise.   Swift, West, and Conger, bore with you
the heat and burden of the day for a few years and then
went early to their reward.   Bergen, Prentice, McMullen,
Goodell,   Holyoke,   Williams,   Dunn,   Weeks,   Willard,

Leonard, and Gary, are cherished in your memories as brothers beloved. Ferris, Bunce, Waters, and Gale, were strong pillars in the edifice you were rearing. But they, too, having finished their work, have gone to their rest. Nor will you forget Spencer, whom you first learned to love as a pious, active Christian pupil in your Academy, and afterward as a minister, honored of God, in leading many souls among you to the Saviour.

Others, who were for a time identified with you, have been called to other fields, and still live to labor elsewhere for the same cause. Among this class the names of Kellogg, Foote, Parker, and Blanchard, will always be prominent in your grateful recollections. May they long live to serve God and their generation as faithfully and successfully as they did with you. Mr. Kellogg had, from the beginning, aided the interests of the colony by his judicious counsels and his liberal pecuniary assistance. While he was President of the College, and while pastor of the Church, his whole heart, influence, and resources were enlisted in putting forward the interests of the colony, and in accomplishing its grand designs. His unselfish and magnanimous services deserve a lasting remembrance.

How wonderful has been the period of time, covered by your enterprise! What changes have transpired; what progress has been made in the useful arts, in the facilities of travel, and of transmitting intelligence! What growth of our country has been witnessed; what progress in our State within these thirty years. Well do you remember the political parties, and the political questions of thirty years ago. Where are they now? You remember the first votes you gave for an anti-slavery ticket. It seemed a day of small things on your side, but now your principles govern Congress, and rule the Nation. You remember those anti-slavery prayer meetings in the old Academy. Look which way you would for help to the slave, you could see only a dead wall high as Heaven. No door of hope was opened, but you believed that he who opened the Red Sea for the deliverance of his ancient people from oppression, could bring Liberty to our oppressed millions, with a mighty hand and an outstretched arm. You there prayed in faith, and by terrible things in righteousness God has answered you. "Jehovah has triumphed, his people are free." In view of what you have been permitted to witness in your day and generation, what may you not hope for in the future! This world is to be disenthralled, reclaimed, and regenerated. The bright visions of prophecy are to be realized. All shall know the Lord, and the earth shall be filled with His glory. As you close up your earthly labors, let it be in the full confidence that the Kingdom of God shall universally prevail; and in thankfulness that you have been permitted to do something to prepare the way for its coming and triumph.

STATISTICAL PAPER.

Business here began in 1835, with the purchase of 10,746,81-100 acres of land for $14,821,10-100; which, with the expenses of exploration, amounted to $16,559,7-100. In 1836 colonists began to take possession, and to build log cabins at Henderson Grove.

During that season building was the principal business of our Pioneer Fathers. Within a year "Log City" was of some renown. Like other cities with room enough in the great world outside—"Log City" had too great a population for its accommodations. Hence three or four families were crowded into a single cabin. One Philemon Phelps, not following the fashions of the "city," went out in the country in the autumn of '36, and on the open prairie built the first frame house; a house known in "modern times" as the old "Holyoke house." It stood on the lot now covered by Mr. Mathews' new brick store, occupied by Mr. Hawkinson, on Main street, east of Prairie. Besides building cabins the colonists, during that summer, raised a little corn, a few potatoes and garden vegetables on the "colony farm," purchased a few cows, and went seventy miles to mill. During the cold winter of 1836-7 those men and women had a good time amid their many privations, to meditate on something good for this portion of Illinois.

With the spring of '37 came new families and an increase of business. Geo. Avery built the second frame house, which was afterwards moved out into the world to the lot now occupied by his present residence of brick. The old house, still stands across the way a little east of its former position, a relic of olden times, covered now as then with "Hoosier boards"—boards rived and shaved about a yard in length. During the summer, "The Prairie" says Mr. Gale "was the theater of a busy activity in the erection of buildings and opening of farms." Mr. Gale's statement that the Academy building was erected during this year (1837) must be a mistake; for the account books of the College show that it could not have been commenced till about June, nor completed before December of 1838.

A settlement had been fairly made; it consisted of those who came in 1836 —173 individuals, and those who came in the spring of 1837—59 individuals— total 232. Of these 165 or 71 per cent. are still living; of those then married nearly 60 per cent. are still living; of those then unmarried over 80 per cent.

These are remarkable facts; those families had been accustomed to the comforts of good Eastern homes. Here they lived in log cabins made of green timber, in one case without a floor, and with several families in a cabin, experiencing a winter so unusually cold that old "Hoosiers" and "Suckers" insisted that the Yankees brought it along with them.

Then, too, some of these men had passed the middle of life. One, Mr. Chambers, was fifty years old, and yet, after thirty years, 70 per cent. are still living. Of men then regarded as within the shadows of age, we have now with us, Deacons Simmons, Tompkins, and Chambers. Long—long—may the good men remain—bright lights in the Church of God. A few years after the settlement of this colony, a gentleman, in a stage coach pronounced all Illinois so unhealthy that there was not a place in it where a family of children could be raised. Mr. W. Selden Gale replied to him: "In the place where I live, fifty-three children were born in the first two years of the settlement, of whom fifty-two are living."

It is not easy to realize that we have among us so large a number of men and women who remember when between the high ground known as the "Knox place," two and a half-miles south-east of us, and Henderson Grove, three and a half-miles north-west; there was nothing but wild prairie grass and rosin weed, not a tree or shrub, nothing to obstruct the vision, excepting the cabin of Mr. Luther Gay, a little this side of the grove, a low cabin, yet, as standing out on a naked prairie, it so loomed up that for years it was called the " *Light-house.*"

Those Pioneers were mostly Christians, and strictly temperate in all their habits. Their remarkable longevity asserts that temperance and godliness are profitable unto all things. Besides, these Pioneers had a great idea; they came for a good work, and were cheerful and happy amid their trials—never happier—so they say; and hence, like the older Pilgrims, they were of such stuff as not, because of trials, to wish themselves back again. Such men had a right to live; a right resting on a Divine promise.

The population of Galesburg in 1846 was about 800; in 1856—4000; and in 1866—8000, or, including the township, 9000.

Galesburg has had a healthy growth,

Half a township in 1835 cost............ $16,559	On the same basis assessments in
Total assessments in 1849.................. 64,945	1866 would be.....................$1,600,00
" " " 1855.................. 399,700	

This property estimated at its full value, would amount to at least $5,000,000.

The lot on which stands the store of Innes, Murdoch & Co., 66x112 feet, cost them $7000.

The mercantile business of Galesburg was commenced in the spring of 1837 by C. S. Colton, in a log cabin at the Grove. After a few months he removed to the building which he had erected for his dwelling and store on the corner of the public square, now occupied by his large brick block.

In that store he did most of the business of the town for ten years. A portion of that old store now stands on Chambers street between Main and North, revealing through the paint the name, "C. S. Colton" on one end, and on the street side, "Books, Stationery, Paints, etc., etc." In its chimney are some of the first brick made in Galesburg. Knoxville and Henderson were *the* places for trade during those years. For a long time if one wanted a piece of stove pipe he was obliged to go to Knoxville, perhaps to Farmington, and sometimes even for thread and needles.

In 1840 Mr. Colton went into the pork trade; and collected from the two counties of Knox and Warren, 192 hogs—all he could buy. These were driven to Warsaw, slaughtered and shipped to New Orleans, at a loss of ten per cent. In 1841 he purchased 1250, and made nothing. In 1842 the standard price of hogs was one dollar and fifty cents a hundred. There were no beef cattle to be had. Dealers from Ohio bought and drove off the steers, as dealers from this State have gone to Arkansas and Texas for young stock to be driven home and fatted for market. Wheat was carted to Chicago and sold at 45 to 50cts per bushel.

In the meantime Mr. Chambers opened a store on the corner of the Square, now occupied by Olmsted & Downs. Then followed several unsuccessful attempts at the mercantile business; till Mr. Johnson, of Knoxville, established a branch store here. Then came the Willards who built up a good business.

During the second decade the business of the place was constantly increasing with the tide of population, and growing prosperity of the College. At the end of this period all were alive, many were building air castles, some were running wild with speculation. A brilliant bubble had been blown all over this Western country. Great cities were about to spring out of the ground; everybody was soon to become rich. Railroads were to run in every direction; and Galesburg become a great city. How that great bubble burst in 1857 is well remembered, and the depression that followed; with the embarrassments and losses growing out of the miserable "wild cat" banks and "stump tail" currency which so cursed this State.

During the last decade the business of our city has had a marked growth. The following figures, obtained from the U. S. Assessor, or directly from business parties, though given in round numbers, closely approximate to the actual amount of business done here in twelve months:

Stock and Produce trade	$1,600,000	Agricultural articles	$125,000
Dry Goods	545,000	Drugs, etc	60,000
Cloths and Clothing	290,000	Crockery (outside Grocery stores)	12,000
Boots and Shoes (outside of Dry Good stores)	35,000	Musical Instruments	40,000
		Sewing Machines	5,000
Fancy Goods and Toys	47,000	Books and Stationery	30,000
Groceries	460,000	Lumber, 5,000,000 feet	185,000
Hardware	154,000	Leather	18,000

Amount, exclusive of many smaller interests...$3,606,000

MANUFACTURES :

	NO. OF MEN EMPLOYED.	WAGES.	PRODUCTS.
Wagons and Plows	50	$35,000	$53,000
Corn Planters	150	* 96,000	$200,000
Sugar Mill, Hay Press, Valve and Foundry Establishments }	100	72,000	440,000
Furniture	22	12,000	45,000
(Including both manufactured and sold) } †			
Harness, Shoes, Household Goods	41	26,000	80,937
Brick (part of a year)	40	8,500	20,000
Preparing Hemp for Market	25	10,000	25,000
Marble Head Stones			11,000
Pumps			6,787
Candy			1,668
Sorghum, 14 000 gallons			14,000
Soap			25,000
Gents' Clothing			60,000
Millinery			40,000
Photographs......$12 000.....Picture Frames......$4 000			16,000

Total $1,038,392

As the party of Hugh Conger and Nehemiah West were approaching the chosen site for their colony, on the first of June, 1836, they stopped for the night near what is now called Victoria. They were short of provisions. The family where they called had no meal. Corn was ground in a hand mill, and "corn dodgers" made for supper. The next day dealing out their scanty supplies to the younger members of the party, they made their way, weary and hungry, to Henderson Grove, gathered up what they could for supper from the Hoosier families scattered through the "timber ;" and took their first meal from a table, consisting of a door from an old Hoosier cabin, resting on boxes. There was so little wheat in this region then that a colonist in some instances spent a week in gathering up half a dozen bushels of it; and then spent another week in carrying it to Andover, (thirty miles) or further to Oquaka and waiting his turn for his "grist," or even seventy miles to a steam mill at Pekin. There was indeed a mill nearer, "Roger's mill," more recently known as "Olmsted's." But in dry times it could not grind. Now, if you wish it, mills right at your door can grind for you 1,000 bushels in twenty-four hours. When all running, our mills grind daily 400 bushels of wheat, and 100 bushels of corn ; proceeds for a year about $250,000. There were slaughtered for our consumption last year 1760 beef cattle ; 859 sheep ; 443 hogs ; making the business of our meat markets amount to $100,000.

The growth of our city is shown by the increase of its *Post Office business.* A newspaper paragraph recently stated that among the worthy deeds which an aged couple had never done was the *mailing* of a *letter.*

---

* For eight months. During the summer months many of these men work as carpenters.
† Some of the furniture of the Pioneers was easily made, as a "spring bedstead" with but one post. Taking the corner of a log cabin, bore holes in the logs for three corners, set up a post for the fourth, then with the sides and ends set in and fastened, lay across "Hoosier boards," with a good *spring* to them and you have a luxury as compared with a "*puncheon* bed." The rule for travellers in the early days was one puncheon to a man. The story is that a company was so crowded one night, that they could lie only on one side; and as one rose in the night, the rest improving the chance for relief, turned back, so that on seeking his puncheon again, the man up could get in only as he waked the whole row and set them up edgewise.

They had *existed.* So have Egyptian mummies. A friend of mine was asked not long ago, in North Carolina, if he thought the United States Government would ever catch Jefferson Davis. Semi-civilized communities have little use for mails. As communities rise in civilization they read and write, and still rise as they increase their correspondence.

The business of this office has always been large for the population. The colonists for a year went to Knoxville for their mails; and brought them thence once a week on horseback. During the winter of 1837–8, the people of "Log City" took their letters from the window-sill of Rev. Mr. Gale; and paid twenty-five cents for a letter from the East, and this for each separate piece of paper, however light or small. It was not long before the colonists rejoiced in a semi-weekly and then a tri-weekly mail. When Mr. Wm. H. Holcomb, of Knoxvile, advertised his stage to run from Peoria to Oquawka, and touch at certain flourishing villages, Galesburg was not named.

After much difficulty the colonists obtained an office, and a mail direct. The mails were not heavy in those days, consisting only of a few letters, a few copies of the New York Observer, Evangelist, and New York Express, bringing the news two or three weeks old. Mr. W. Selden Gale, who was postmaster in 1850–3, remembers when on a Monday morning, an unusually large mail of one hundred letters was sent off. The income of the office did not probably exceed $1500 during either of these years.

The returns from this office for the quarter ending March 31st, 1866, as furnihsed by the postmaster, C. E. Carr, Esq., through his chief clerk, Mr. George Colville, present the following facts:

```
"Quarterly sales of stamps and stamped envelopes...................................................$2,455,07
    "      amount of unpaid postage collected.................................................... 230,60
    "        "      "  postage upon regular newspapers and magazines...................... 95,94
```

Upwards of 2,000 regular newspapers are received weekly, from all parts of the country, for delivery to subscribers. Among religious papers the Inde. pendent stands first, with 110 subscribers. Number of boxes rented nearly 1,000.

```
Gross receipts of Postoffice quarterly (average)...............................................$3,021,05
Net       "      to U. S. after defraying expenses of office......................................... 1,925,30
Number of letters received per week for delivery............................................ 5,083
    "     "    "      "      "  quarter for delivery....................................66,079
And for a year considerably over a quarter of a million.
```

Of this number are delivered 981 out of every thousand; the remainder, less than two per cent. of the whole, being advertised as "unclaimed," and eventually finding their way back to the writers through the Dead Letter office.

The number of letters sent from the Galesburg postoffice, will average, all the year 'round, the same as that of those received—from five to six thousand weekly. About the same number as in the case of letters received, fail from various causes to reach the parties addressed, and are returned to the writers through the Dead Letter office.

The money order system is of recent date; but the business is steadily on the increase. For the quarter ending March 31st, 1866, the aggregate amount of the orders issued (all in small sums) footed up $1,974,49·100—of orders paid, $1,110,26.

The office ranks as the third or fourth in the State, and the literary character of our people—as shown in the items of letters received and sent—will challenge any town of like size to produce its equal.   Many letters also go directly through the mail car.

Besides what comes through the postoffice, news agents distribute

Daily Papers...270 | Weekly Miscellaneous Pamphlets............. 50
Weekly Political Papers.....................200 | Monthly Magazines................................250
  "   Illustrated Papers.....................300 |
Total of different publications regularly taken outside of the Postoffice.......................1,070

During the late war the citizens of Galesburg expended from $4,000 to $5,000 a year for daily news.

OUR RAIL ROADS.

Not till long after the settlement of this place was there any railroad west of the Alleghanies.   Our Pioneer Fathers were about eight weeks coming hither from Vermont; six weeks from Central New York.   For several years a merchant's trip to New York took eighteen or twenty days; four to six days to Chicago.   A trip to Chicago and back, with a loaded wagon, required two weeks.   When the Michigan canal was opened you seemed quite near to Chicago; you could reach that village—as it then was—by stage to Peoria; steamboat to La Salle; then by canal boat; in forty-eight hours—about the time now required to reach New York.

From the slow and hard wagon, to the stage and steamer, was a great change. But what a change from the coach to one of Pullman's magnificent $20,000 sleeping cars—splendid as a palace—easy as a cradle—gently rocking one to sleep at ten o'clock in the evening—giving him pure air to breathe all night— enabling him to rise in Chicago with the sun—wash and prepare for business as if at a first-class hotel.

The first railroad idea here was for a track to Peoria.   Fifteen years ago a charter was obtained for a road from Peoria to Oquawka, to run two and a half miles south of Galesburg; with a station at Knoxville and another eight miles distant, on the county line, leaving this place—nowhere, but five miles from Knoxville.   Our citizens plead for a station at this point, and offered to take stock to the amount of $20,000.   They thought only of reaching Peoria, and a market by rail and Illinois river.   There was also a charter for a road from Quincy to La Salle—in *words* not to run *East* of Knoxville, and in *thought* not to run *West* of that place.   Again Galesburg was left out in the cold.

Despairing of accommodation from either road, if ever built, the people here determined to reach the Rock Island road at Sheffield.   A correspondence was opened; meetings were held; an organization formed; a charter secured, small subscriptions obtained; the route surveyed, and Mr. C. M. Carr put into the field as agent to wake up the people.   Still the enterprise dragged.   Many stood looking towards Peoria.   The Rock Island company failed to "know their day."

But earnest men and stern difficulties were· educating the public mind and stretching it on beyond Sheffield to Aurora—the terminus of the Chicago and Aurora road—and preparing for a strike direct to Chicago. Fortune turned on a single incident, a casual meeting in Boston, of Mr. C. S. Colton with Mr. Grimes, of Iowa—now U. S. Senator—and Mr. Wadsworth, President of the Chicago and Aurora road. Thus was secured important aid at each end of the proposed road. Soon after this, Mr. Brooks, President of the Michigan Central, and Mr. Joy, the first and present President of our road, were enlisted. Eastern capital was now obtained, and the road made certain. The first charter was enlarged; the road was built and, in 1854, opened. Finally, in order that the Peoria and Oquawka road might be finished, the "Military Tract" road, as our road was first called, had to buy it. The C. B. & Q., now has 400 miles of road.

This passage of history is given to show what Galesburg enterprise had to do to secure this great road.

The railroad business at this point is important. Taking the month of May as an average month, the amount of Merchandise shipped from this point during the last year was 40,831,176 lbs., on which was charged a freight of $104,554,64.

Our stock and grain dealers ship largely from other points. At this station the shipments for the year ending June 1st, 1866, have been

Grain	400 000 bushels	Sheep	200 head
Cattle	2 600 head	Horses	50 "
Hogs	9 000 "	Broom Corn	685 000 lbs.

Cash collected on freight received, for the year...$136,882,67.

This department has employed seventeen hands, and paid for their labor $10,200 for the year.

It would be a fact of interest, if known, how many, during the first ten years after the settlement of the place, started on a journey.

The number of passengers by rail from Galesburg in the year ending April 30th, 1862, was 28,651; in the year ending April 30th, 1866, was 82,555. Increase of travel in four years, 53,904.

The following statement from Superintendent Hitchcock shows the increase of business in the train department:

TRAIN MEN EMPLOYED AT GALESBURG, MAY, 1856.

	NO.	AMOUNT.
Conductors	7	354 50
Baggage Man	1	35 00
Brakemen	7	182 49
Total amount	15	$571 99

TRAIN MEN EMPLOYED AT GALESBURG, MAY, 1866.

	NO.	AMOUNT.
Passenger Conductors	11	712 36
Freight "	37	2 652 19
Baggage Men	9	430 62
Passenger Brakemen	9	338 05
Freight "	75	3 119 39
Total amount	141	$7 252 61
Amount of wages for twelve months		$87 031 82

The carpenter's department has done a large amount of work. The present extensive Freight House, and Carpenter's Shop, were built in 1855; the large Passenger House in 1856; the Locomotive Repair Shop, 50x150, in 1861-2. The Car Shop was burned and rebuilt, 50x180, in 1863.

At different times other buildings have been erected, as the present office building, storage buildings, and an engine house with stalls for thirty-five engines. This department employed during the fall of 1863 and the year '64, an average of 180 men. It now has an average of seventy-five men, on a yearly pay of $32,200.

Arrangements are being made to dig a large well, sufficient to supply all the water that may be needed for many years, at a cost of from $8,000 to $10,000. Other improvements are contemplated, to meet the demands of the increasing business of the road.

LOCOMOTIVE DEPARTMENT.

The Locomotive department of the C. B. & Q. R. R., at Galesburg, employs from 230 to 240 men of all classes; whose pay ranges from $1 30 to $3 40 per day.

```
Average monthly expenditure for labor.............................................11 311 00
   "       "          "       " material..............................................  4 720 00
   "       "          "       " oil, &c................................................  2 580 00
                                                                         ──────────
                                                                          $18 561 00
```

THE EXPENDITURES FOR THE YEAR ENDING APRIL 30, 1866.

```
Labor on engines.................48 927 81 | Oil and waste on engines.............11 107 80
Material on   "    .................34 319 13 |
   Making a total expense on engines of..........................................$94 354 74
Labor on track, buildings, cars, etc..40 135 63 | Oil & waste used on build'gs, cars... 19 251 23
Material used on   "        "    .......22 160 63 |
                                                                         ──────────
                                                                          $81 547 49
   For Engineers, Firemen, and Wipers, etc., one year.................$46 670 00.
Making a total of Labor...............135 733 44 | Mak'g a total of oil, tallow, rags......30 359 03
   "        "   "  Material..........  56 479 76 |
   Total....................................................................................$222 572 23
```

TRACK DEPARTMENT.

The number of men employed in the Track Department at Galesburg is 60. These are regular men and work steadily the whole year round. Most of these are men with families, and hence probably spend or leave all their earnings in Galesburg, thus materially contributing to the wealth of the place.

The aggregate pay of these men was $30,475,00. In addition to these regular men, there were employed in Galesburg, in the construction and extension of side-tracks, etc., etc., twenty men for about seven months, at an expense for labor, teams, in grading, etc., etc., of about $7,500,00; a good share of which was paid to men who are permanent residents here.

There were about one and one-half miles of new side-track and extensions to side-tracks laid in Galesburg during the past year. The cost of material for these constructions was $18,000.

THE CAR DEPARTMENT.

This department has employed during the year, on an average, 81 1-6 men; average pay per month, $47,09; amounting in the year to $45,863,53. Value of material used in repairs, $79,107,65; total, $124,971,18.

TELEGRAPH.

When this prairie was purchased for a town, Prof. Morse had not asked Congress for aid to enable him to test his great discovery. Not till 1844 was the telegraph put into successful operation between Washington and Baltimore. Mr. Tubbs furnishes the following statement:

" In May, 1856, the Illinois and Mississippi Telegraph Company owned one wire from Chicago to Burlington—207 miles—with ten offices. Receipts of Galesburg office about one-fifth their present amount. In May, 1866, the Illinois and Mississippi Telegraph Company owned one wire from Chicago to Keokuk—250 miles ; another from Chicago to Mendota—85 miles—thence over the Illinois Central Railroad to Dunleith.

" The Chicago, Burlington, and Quincy Railroad (the only road in the West owning their own telegraph) have one wire over the entire length of their road and its branches ; a second wire from Chicago to Mendota, which will be extended to Galesburg this fall, (1866); a third wire for the accommodation of the general offices in Chicago from their passenger depot, foot of Lake street, via South Branch Freight Depot to their extensive docks.

"Total number of miles of wire owned by the road, 513 ; total number miles on line of road, 805 ; number of offices, 59.

" We claim as complete a system of Train Dispatching as any road in the country. The present business of the road could not be done over a single track without it. Since its adoption—two years ago—not a wheel has been off the track, chargeable either directly or indirectly to it.

"The number of messages received and sent at the Galesburg office in May, 1856, was 176 ; in May, 1866, 11,780. Office employees, June, 1856, operators one, messengers one ; June, 1866, operators and train dispatchers, six ; battery and delivery clerks, two. Office salaries June, 1856, $30,00 ; June, 1866, $721,00. "

These figures are full of meaning. Many a dispatch contained a great history—on single telegram fortunes turn. In no other so brief a form is there, or can there be, condensed so much of thought, emotion, and business, as in the telegrams of the day.

EXPRESS.

Another marked fact of a kindred character is found in the EXPRESS BUSINESS at this point. The business done at this office for the month of January, 1855, amounted to $78,00. This was the first year of the Express Business at this point. The amount in the month of January, 1866, or eleven years later, is $2,477, an increase of $2,399.

Taking January as a fair average, the business for the year amounts to $29,724.

Business now, could not dispense with the Telegraph or Express.

Thanks to the gentlemenly officials of the road for aid, cheerfully rendered, in obtaining these facts.

Mr. Sellon, in a brief history of Galesburg published in 1857, states that the

whole number of men employed in the several departments of the road, at
Galesburg, was 145.   The number now employed, including Express men, is
634. Their annual wages amounting to $364,694,12.   This Railroad business
itself reveals much in regard to the business of the city.   It is not strange
that the stock of the C. B. & Q. R. R., which in 1860 was only 38 cents, is now
in 1866, 115 cents.

As this portion of our State is rapidly developing; as railroad lines are
extending Westward from Burlington and Quincy to the Missouri river, to be
connected with the great National Pacific Road—who will grow bold enough
to predict the value of the C. B. & Q., stock in 1876?

Many minor interests have not been looked into for lack of time.   But in the
facts here given we have some results worthy of thought.   Using round numbers for convenience, we have of laborers—mostly mechanical (including the
R. R. men) eleven hundred, with wages amounting to $660,000.   We have an
aggregate of business

Stock and Produce.........................$1 600 000	Flouring Mills.............................$250 000
Mercantile............................... 2 006 000	Meat Markets............................. . 100 000
Manufactures.............................. 1 038 000	
Total..$4 994 000		

It is fair to state the aggregate as $5,000,000, exclusive of many smaller
branches of business, and also of the heavy Railroad business.

Our business though increasing, is sound and healthy.   Speculation for the
future is not the work of these figures.   They give the facts of the present.
What now exists is far beyond the anticipations of the good men and women
who looked over this prairie thirty years ago.   But not for gain, not for anything less than a sound Christian education, did our Pioneer Fathers come.

This should still be the great end.   What we do to build up noble characters
in ourselves, and in the generations to come, in the millions to dwell on this
old magnificent "Military Tract," is the great thing.

In 1836–7, a school was taught at the Grove, both in the common and academic branches, by Prof. Losey and Miss Lucy Gay.   Another school was opened
in the winter of 1837 by Miss Fanny Hitchcock, (Mrs. Hayner) in a small house
—erected for this purpose—on the farm of Mr. Leonard Chappel, East of Mr.
Samuel Hitchcock's.   A singing school was also there taught.

Prof. Churchill states that " a public school was opened in the winter of
1839, in the second story of the Academy building—then just completed—the
one now occupied by Mr. Nelson as a furniture store—at the time it stood on the
corner of Main and Cherry, where the First National Bank is to be built this
summer.

"The first teacher was Mr. Van Meter, the man who has been so long at the
head of the Howard Mission, N. Y. City.   In a short time it was removed to a
store building owned by Matthew Chambers, fronting what is now the Public
Square—then wild prairie.   In 1839 or '40, the first public school house was
built under the direction of C. S. Colton.   As the floor was inclined, all the
old scholars will remember this building as a capital place to slide down hill in
the spaces between the seats.   Among the many teachers who held rule in this

house from 1840 to 1850, were Eli Farnham, Esq., James H. Noteware, since Superintendent of Public Schools for Kansas, Mr. McCall, for many years a teacher in the South, and recently deceased, Mr. Marshal De Long, Mr. H. Guston, Mr. Deberard, Geo. Churchill, and ladies not a few. About the year 1850 the district was divided and new school houses were built to accommodate the rising generation. This sub-division went on till 1856, when there were in the town eight districts."

During the year 1856, "these districts"—says Mr. J. B. Roberts, the present Superintendent of Public Schools—"were consolidated with a view to more efficient management and a better classification of the schools. No well devised measures for the promotion of these objects, however, were attempted until the year 1859. These measures were but partially successful, from the fact that the Board of Directors were limited in their powers, and still more in the means at their command. What could be done under these disabilities and with miserably poor and insufficient school accommodations, was done. In the year 1861, the schools were organized under a special charter from the Legislature, greatly enlarging the powers of the School Board, which now consists of six instead of three members. In the year 1865, these powers were still further enlarged by an amendment to the charter. The School Board have it now in their power, by an enlightened and liberal policy, to make the public schools no less the pride and honor of the city than its higher institutions of learning have been in the past.

"During the School year just closed, there have been taught between fifteen and sixteen hundred different pupils. The average membership has been from nine hundred to a thousand. The number of teachers employed in '64 and '65 was eighteen. During the past year the number has been less, owing to limited school accommodations, as rooms previously occupied could no longer be rented. The public school buildings of Galesburg will seat 596 pupils. It will readily be understood why several of the schools have had only half-day sessions. The new edifice, when completed, will increase the number of sittings by about seven hundred. This building, aside from being the best proportioned and most comely structure of any kind in the city, will be, in its internal arrangements and appointments as perfect as possible. It will contain ten large school rooms, a hall for general exercises, public entertainments, and some smaller rooms to be used as recitation rooms and offices. The system of ventilation is novel, but proved by experience to be the most perfect yet devised. It is calculated that the entire body of air in each school room can be changed every twenty minutes without opening a door or window. It is expected that this building will be completed within the present year, at a cost of $40,000. Its stone tablet bearing the date "1866," will be looked upon by generations to come as marking the completion of one of the noblest enterprises in the history of our city."

Prairie College (now Knox) was THE OBJECT for which Christian men and women organized and built up this colony.

This institution is still in its infancy, having graduated its first class just twenty years ago. Still it has done a good work, as the following statistics furnished by Prof. Churchill, plainly show:

Decades.	Graduates.	Seniors.	Juniors.	Sophomores.	Freshmen.	Scientific.	Total Collegians.	Lady Graduates.	Seniors.	Middlers.	Juniors.	Total Lady Collegiates.	Gents' Academic.	Ladies Academic.	Total Academic.	Total of all Departments.
1837 to 1846 Inclusive.	9	9	15	29	56		109						699	626	1325	1434
1847 to 1856 Inclusive.	60	71	101	128	199		499	40	60	85	73	218	1471	1149	2620	3337
1857 to 1866 Inclusive.	53	58	73	107	149	38	425	78	102	125	107	334	1213	944	2157	2916
1837 to 1866 Inclusive.	131	138	189	264	404	38	1033	118	162	210	180	552	3383	2719	6102	7687

Of the grand catalogue total of 7687 students, I estimate that there have been at least 5,000 different persons. The academic department was opened in 1837. First freshmen class in 1841; first class graduated in 1846; first class in the Seminary graduated in 1851.

```
Greatest number in all departments for any one year was........................442 in 1858
   "      "     "   the College     "     "    "   "    "   ....................... 59 " 1855
Least number in College for any one year since 1847 was....................... 32 " 1865
Average number in College for 1st Decade.....36 1-3......Seminary.....   ......Academy...132 1-3
   "      "     "    "       " 2d     "       49 9-10        "       31 1-7        "        215 7-10
   "      "     "    "       " 3d     "       42 1-2         "       33 2-5        "        203 2-5
   "      "     "    "       " three Decades 42 41-45   "    32 19-70        "        203 2-5
```

Of the 131 gentlemen graduates eleven have died; thirty-eight are ministers; twenty-four lawyers; six physicians; fourteen professors and teachers; three foreign missionaries; three State Agents—Home Missionary Societies; three foreign consuls; two Brevet-Brigadier Generals; forty-five officers and privates in army of volunteers. Some eight or ten have been members of the State Legislature, and others are bankers, merchants, manufacturers or farmers.

For a dozen years after graduating its first class, this College was realizing the great idea of the colonists, was the main object of interest, and the power most felt in this community. With a growing population, increasing wealth, improved public schools, why should not the College have continued rising and kept pace with all the other real interests of the place?

The catalogue of Lombard University—just published gives the following summary:

```
Collegiate Department......Seniors 2......Juniors  ......Sophomores 4......Freshmen  3        9
Scientific      "      ......     "    2......   "    1......              "     14       17
Ladies' Collegiate "  ......          "    ......   "    1...... First year .....         10       11
                      ( Ancient and Modern Languages.............................. 46 )
Preparatory Department,{ Higher  English.......................................... 113 }    207
                      ( Common     "   ............................................... 48 )
```

244

. Another educational organization, "The Young Men's Library Association," deserves mention. This association was founded in January, 1860, (a preliminary organization, formed in 1858, was merged in this,) and has 250 members and a Library of 2850 volumes. All are entitled to its privileges upon the payment of a small sum. It is useful and prosperous. Its Library, managed as efficiently as now by Prof. Hurd, with annual additions, may, in future, be an honor to the city, as well as a blessing to many generations of young men.

At the end of the first decade the principal object of general interest was this house of worship, which, though unfinished, was occupied in the summer of 1846. Here for twenty years the people of this town have held most of their public meetings, for lectures, concerts, and a great variety of purposes. To fit it for service for another decade it needs for improvements within and without, an expenditure of a few thousand dollars.

At the end of the second decade the main College buildings were rising up to adorn the city. Now the main building is that for the High School.

For the beautiful trees now shading this house, we are much indebted to a former pastor, Rev. C. M. Tyler.

Our city, which, ten years ago gloried in but few trees besides the Locust, is now assuming the charming appearance of an Eastern village with its older trees, of Elm and Maple. More Elms, gentlemen! more Elms! for grace and majesty combined.

Another generation will marvel that not till 1866 was there an enclosure or a tree in the centre of the Public Square, nothing on the bare earth but the Liberty Pole and city scales. Another marked improvement made in the last decade is in *side walks*. The first walk was built around "Colton's Block."

Many amusing stories have been told of the loss of rubbers, shoes, and even of boots in the mud of those days, and of persons becoming not lost but "fixtures." In 1856 but few short spaces were covered with good walks. They now extend in all directions quite to the city limits, amounting in all to thirty miles in length, and costing not far from $50,000.

A people of Puritan blood and spirit, with deep religious convictions and anti-slavery sentiments, and familiar with the business of the "Underground Railroad" would be sure to make a good record in a war for the salvation of the Republic.

The following figures furnished by Miss M. A. West, make a fair show of the patriotism of Galesburg:

No. of men enlisted in the township......1200	Amount of bounty paid...............$23 950 00
No. of men died in the army..................... 100	Am't p'd by city to Soldiers families 16 000

Total...$39 950 00

Galesburg Soldier's Aid Society for soldiers, and soldier's families, disbursed stores and money:

In 1862...............................$2 397 82	Till August 1865.........................$2 604 76
In 1863............................. .... 2 686 66	
In 1864............................... 5 806 89	Total from Galesburg S. A. Society.$13 586 13
Galesburg paid to the Sanitary and Christian Commissions, aside from the S. A. S...$6 614 73	
For Soldiers and Freedmen's Reading... 2 199 10	

To all..$32 340 16

The facts of our *Church History* demand more space than can be afforded now, and will claim attention next February—when the First Church will be thirty years old.

An incident in our early history is worthy of record. A Mr. Davis had enclosed forty acres of land, with the intention of "entering" it. But the land was included with the "entries" of the Purchasing Committee. So also was a farm of a hundred and twenty acres, occupied by a Mr. Lander. They thought the Yankees were sharp as "speculators," and felt in no way pleasantly about it. But not long after the question was started at "a raising," whether the right to the forty acres of Mr. Davis would not be relinquished. The suggestion seemed reasonable, and was adopted. Whereupon Mr. Lander was encouraged to make a similar application, and was successful. "Well, now," said they, and the settlers about the Grove, "let the Yankees come· *They may educate our children.*" Who shall assign a market value to that high minded transaction? With the confidence and good will of a community, an institution of learning may prosper, but not without such sympathy.

This paper may not be closed without the names of two business men: the one removed in the early part of this last decade, and the other at its close. Silas Willard, and Albert G. Watkins. Other good men have here toiled and rested, but for none does the public heart cherish a profounder respect or deeper love.

Greatness is in the end aimed at, and in the spirit with which business is transacted. The greatness of our Pioneer—as of our Pilgrim Fathers—was in the greatness of the faith and purpose with which they undertook "something good for mankind and God's glory in these remote parts of the earth."

Let all our business men rise to the same hight, and be crowned with a like glory when all use of figures shall have passed away.

FESTIVAL AND EVENING EXERCISES.

AT the close of the afternoon exercises the audience adjourned to the chapel for supper. This room— recently refitted—was tastefully decorated for the occasion. Across the wall, at the upper end, ran the words, in evergreen letters, " He hath led us, by a right way, to a city of habitation." Over the entrance was a pyramid of flowers, having on one side a model of a log house, with the words, "Log City, 1836," and on the other a modern house representing "Galesburg, 1866." The houses were transparent, and when illuminated appeared finely. Festoons of evergreens, gracefully connecting the side walls with the chandelier, adorned the center. The tables were as inviting as shining silver, fragrant flowers, delicious viands, and attentive waiters could make them.

The old folks' table was the rallying point for old settlers, and a happy group they seemed as they shook hands and laughed over reminiscences of the good old times. Over it presided one, who thirty years ago came here a bride, now assisted by the brides of her two sons. Outside, under a bower between the chapel and gate, strawberries, ice-cream, and lemonade were strong attractions; while under the refreshing shade of the trees the old folks renewed old friendships, and the young folks formed new ones, till eight o'clock in the evening, when Prof. Fuhrman, who presided at the organ during all the exercises, recalled the assembly to the Church, where addresses were made by Rev. H. Foote, first pastor of the Church, who gave some pleasing reminiscences of early times—of the way people became "fixtures" in the mud—and how he had been shipwrecked in Cedar Fork—running his wagon tongue into the mud, so as nearly "to strike ile,"—leaving nothing to be seen of the wagon but the shadow of the end board; by Rev. Geo. W. Duffield, Jr., pastor of the Second Presbyterian Church, who in a happy speech, affectionately claimed a place in the brotherhood; by R. S. Hanneman, Esq., of Knoxville, who with J. G. Sanborn and their wives, were first to offer to the infant colony the right hand of fellowship from her five year old sister, who now owns the court house and poor farm. Also by several old settlers: Joseph Holyoke, Eli Farnham, J. G. West, Prof. H. E. Hitchcock, Marcus Belden, telling how he had "carted" water to run a mill at Knoxville, C. S. Colton, who explained the *one per cent. profits* of the early days. Prof. Churchill introduced a choir of old settlers, who had not sung together for twenty years. They sang a piece which they had sung together at a musical Convention held in the old Academy, a quarter of a century ago, and several times during the evening quickened our memories of old times by their music. Letters were read from President Blanchard, Revs. Sanford Richardson, and W. E. Holyoke, expressing their deep interest in the occasion, and their regrets at not being able to be present. The closing address was made by Rev. J. E. Roy, and was a fitting close to the exercises of the day. His tribute to the founders of the town and College was given most heartily, and his sketches of early days were graphic and pleasing.

ERRATA.

Page 4—28th line, for "has," read "have saved."

Page 7—last line, for "1855," read "1835."

Page 30—36th line, for "market," read "a market."

Page 32—3d line, for "locomotive," read "car."

And add at the end of 4th line : "The Locomotive Repair Shop, 60x180 with a wing 60x60."

Page 33— 29th line, for "one, &c.," read " on single telegrams."

Page 34—after the 21st line, the following paragraph should have been inserted :

"For the accommodation of this business we have two Banks—the First National, with a capital of $150,000. Net gain prior to May dividend, $15,022,55. Amount of dividend declared, 6 per cent.; profits over dividend declared, $5,548,90; 5 per cent. retained as tax, $751,13. Second National Bank—capital, $100,000. Net Gain prior to dividend, $8,111,45; amount of dividend declared, $1,795,67 ; 5 per cent. retained as tax, $405,56."

АТАЛА

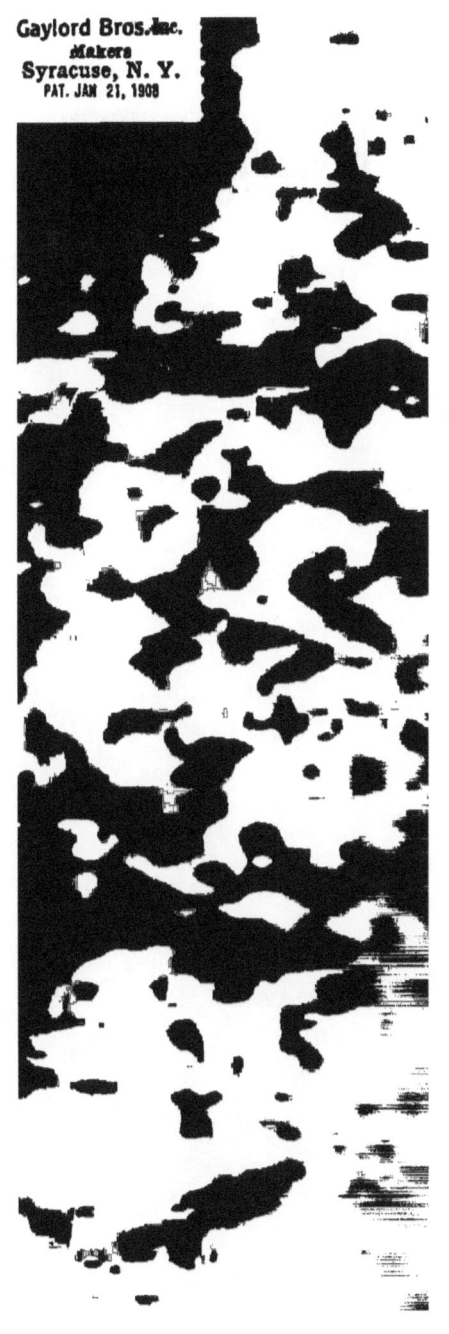